Symbols of America

BALD EAGLE

By Christina Earley

TABLE OF CONTENTS

A Crabtree Seedlings Book

CRABTREE
Publishing Company
www.crabtreebooks.com

School-to-Home Support for Caregivers and Teachers

This book helps children grow by letting them practice reading. Here are a few guiding questions to help the reader with building his or her comprehension skills. Possible answers appear here in red.

Before Reading:

- What do I think this book is about?
  - *I think this book is about bald eagles.*
  - *I think this book is about why the bald eagle is a symbol of the United States.*

- What do I want to learn about this topic?
  - *I want to learn more about why the bald eagle was selected to be a symbol of the United States.*
  - *I want to learn more about bald eagles and their families.*

During Reading:

- I wonder why...
  - *I wonder why a United States spacecraft was named Eagle.*
  - *I wonder why eagles are called bald.*

- What have I learned so far?
  - *I have learned that the presidential flag has a picture of a bald eagle on it.*
  - *I have learned that coins and paper money have impressions of bald eagles on them.*

After Reading:

- What details did I learn about this topic?
  - *I have learned that Benjamin Franklin did not want the bald eagle to be the symbol of the United States.*
  - *I have learned that bald means white.*

- Read the book again and look for the vocabulary words.
  - *I see the word **feathers** on page 6, and the word **laws** on page 8. The other glossary words are found on pages 22 and 23.*

BALD EAGLE

The bald eagle is a **symbol** of America.

This bird lives only in North America.

Most bald eagles in the United States live in Alaska.

Bald eagles are not bald. Their heads have white feathers.

The word “bald” is from the old English word “balde” which means white.

Bald eagles used to be **endangered**.

Now there are **laws** protecting eagles.

The Founding Fathers, the creators of the United States of America, chose the bald eagle as a national symbol in 1782.

Benjamin Franklin, one of the Founding Fathers, did not think bald eagles were a good choice for the national symbol because they steal food from others.

A spacecraft named *Eagle* landed on the Moon.

A symbol for the event shows a bald eagle in space.

The bald eagle can be found on **seals**. These seals are used on important papers.

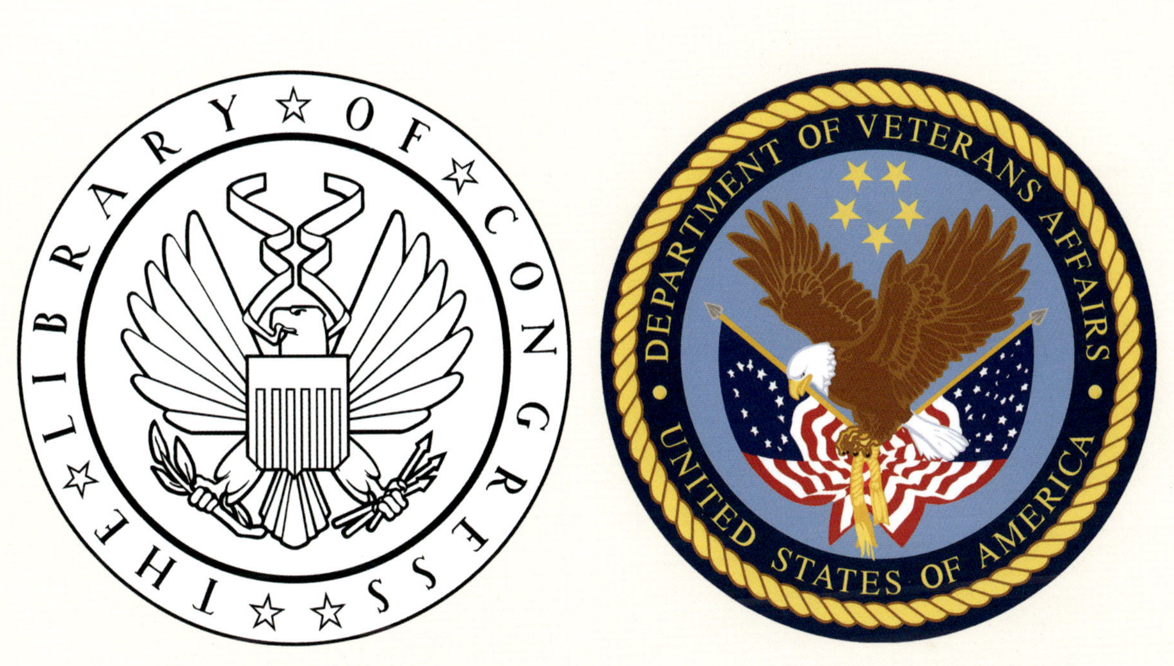

At least 17 branches and departments of the U.S. **government** use the bald eagle on their **official** seals.

Coins and paper money have bald eagles.

Buildings have bald eagles.

The presidential flag has a bald eagle.

There are state flags that use bald eagles.

The bald eagle shows strength and courage.

It is a great symbol of America.

Glossary

endangered (en-DAYN-jrd): Seriously at risk of dying out

government (GUH-vr-muhnt): The group that is in charge of an area

laws (laaz): Rules created by a government

official (uh-FI-shl): Relating to a decision by those in charge

seals (seelz): Items with an individual design stamped on them

symbol (SIM-bl): A thing that represents something else

Index

About the Author

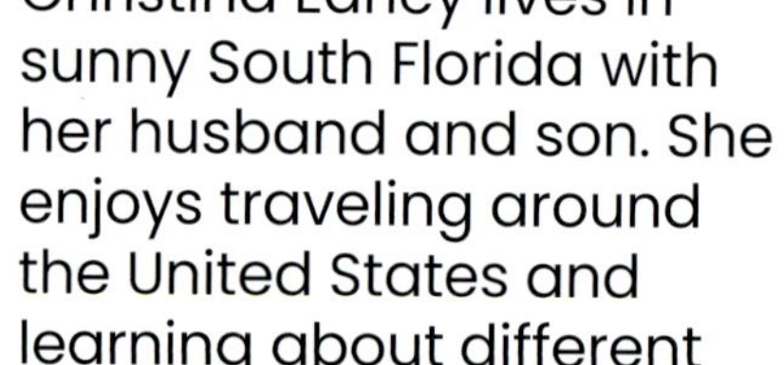

Christina Earley lives in sunny South Florida with her husband and son. She enjoys traveling around the United States and learning about different historical places. Her hobbies include hiking, yoga, and baking.

CRABTREE
Publishing Company

Written by: Christina Earley
Designed by: Kathy Walsh
Proofreader: Petrice Custance

Photographs: Shutterstock: cover: ©Steve Boice; ©MT511, ©dz; Title Pg: ©MT511, ©dz; Pg 4, 6, 8, 11, 12, 14-18 ©MT511; Pg 3 & 23: ©Gianfranco Bella; Pg 4: ©Ad_hominem; Pg 5 ©FloridaStock; Pg 7: ©Ludo KOOS; Pg 9, 22: © Paul Reeves Photography; Pg 10: ©Rosemarie Mosteller; Pg 11: ©Richard Seeley; Pg 12: ©NASA; Pg 13: ©NASA; Pg 14, 15, 23, 24: ©Wiki; Pg 16: ©PhotoVectorStudio, ©kavalenkava; Pg 17: ©Willy Barton; Pg 18 ©Zscout370 at English Wikipedia; Pg 19 @Wiki; Pg 20: ©Brian D Smith;

Library and Archives Canada Cataloguing in Publication
CIP available at Library and Archives Canada

Library of Congress Cataloging-in-Publication Data
CIP available at Library of Congress

Crabtree Publishing Company
www.crabtreebooks.com 1-800-387-7650

Printed in the U.S.A./072022/CG20220201

Published in the United States
Crabtree Publishing
347 Fifth Avenue, Suite 1402-145
New York, NY, 10016

Published in Canada
Crabtree Publishing
616 Welland Ave.
St. Catharines, Ontario L2M 5V6